Smiles

Marcia & David Kaplan
Art by Phil Mendez

The material in this book has been compiled over a long period of time. Many of the sources are unknown to the compilers. We wish to acknowledge the original authors whoever they may be.

Third Printing 1984
Copyright © 1982 by
David E. Kaplan &
Marcia P. Kaplan.
Atlanta, GA., USA

Art by Phil Mendez
Copyright © 1982

ISBN: 0-9617744-1-X

*This book is dedicated to
Ginnie Phillips and Marshall Weaver
who brought smiles to everyone
they touched.*

*Always smile
when you can;
it is
good medicine.*

*I accept life unconditionally.
Life holds so much—so much
to be happy about always.
Most people ask for
happiness on condition.
Happiness can be felt only
if you don't set conditions.*

...Arthur Rubinstein

*Remember the tide
turns at low water,*

as well as high.

Strangers are friends you have yet to meet.

MY LEADER!

*There is nothing
either good
or bad except
that thinking
makes it so.*

...Shakespeare

*To succeed
you must be
easy to start*

and hard to stop.

The will to win

is not worth a nickel

unless you have

the will to prepare.

*It's not
the towering sail
but
the unseen wind
that moves
the ship.*

Life is short but there is always time for courtesy.

...Ralph Waldo Emerson
"Social Arms"

By nature,
man is nearly alike;
by practice,
he gets to be
wide apart.

…Confucius

*Better keep yourself
clean and bright,
you are the window
through which you
must see the world.*

...George Bernard Shaw

*The human mind
doesn't care
what you plant—
success or failure—
but it
will return
what
you plant.*

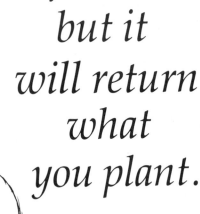

*When someone
says,
"life is hard."
Ask them,
"compared to what?"*

Don't Quit

When things go wrong,
   as they sometimes will,
When the road you're trudging
   seems all uphill,
When the funds are low
   and the debts are high,
And you want to smile,
   but you have to sigh,
When care is pressing you down a bit,
Rest, if you must—but don't you quit.

Life is queer with its twists and turns,
As everyone of us sometimes learns,
And many a "failure" turns about
When he might have won
   had he stuck it out:
Don't give up, though
   the pace seems slow,
You may succeed with another blow.

Often the goal is nearer than
It seems to a faint and faltering man;
Often the struggler has given up
When he might have captured
      the victor's cup;
And he learned too late,
      when the night slipped down,
How close he was to the golden crown.

Success is failure turned inside out—
The silver tint of the cloud of doubt,
And you never can tell
      how close you are,
It may be near when it seems afar;
So stick to the fight
      when you're hardest hit—
It's when things seem worst
      that you mustn't quit.

On two occasions you should learn to keep  *your mouth shut—*

when swimming and when angry.

Your success and happiness lie in you… resolve to keep happy, and your joy and you shall form an invincible host against difficulties.

…Helen Keller

*Genius is the ability
to evade work
by doing something
right the first time.*

...American Salesman

*Don't judge a man
until you have
walked a mile
in his moccasins.*

...C. Geronimo

We have two ends
With a common link;
With one we sit,
With one we think.
Success depends
          on what we use—

Heads we win;

          tails we lose.

*You cannot
push anyone
up the ladder
unless he is willing
to climb himself.*

…Andrew Carnegie

Take time to work,
It is the price of success.
Take time to think,
It is the source of power.
Take time to play,
It is the secret
 of perpetual youth.
Take time to be friendly,
It is the road to happiness.
Take time to love and be loved,
It is the privilege of the gods.
Take time to share.
Life is too short to be selfish.
Take time to laugh,
Laughter is the music
 of the soul.

The loudest boos

always come

from

those in the free seats.

The Value of a Smile

A smile creates happiness
   in the home,
fosters good will
   in business
and is the counter sign
   to friends.

It is rest to the weary,
daylight to the discouraged,
sunshine to the sad
and nature's best antidote
   for trouble.

Yet it cannot be bought,
    begged, borrowed or stolen;
for it is something that is
no earthly good to anyone
    until it is given away.

And if someone is too tired
    to give you a smile
just give them one of yours.
For nobody needs a smile
as much as those who have
    none left to give.

We act as though comfort and luxury were the chief requirements of life when all we need to make us really happy is something to be enthusiastic about.

…Charles Kingsley

*No one ever injured
his eyesight
by looking
on the bright side
of things.*

*He who cuts
his own firewood
is twice warmed.*

You never can tell
by how much noise
the horn makes,
how much gas
is in the tank.

*Everyday
is a little life;
every wakening and
rising a little birth,
every fresh morning
a little youth.*

He who obtains
has nothing,
He who scatters
has everything.

You can be thirty years old or seventy years young. Decide in your favor.

*There's no
traffic jam
on the
extra
mile.*

When love and skill work together, expect a masterpiece.

...*John Ruskin*

*The tail is a dog's
PR department,
a smile is yours!*

You gotta be a man
to play baseball
for a living
but you gotta have
a lot of little boy
in you, too.

… Roy Campenella

There are many ways
of doing things
a casual glance discloses;
Some folks
turn up their sleeves
at work,
and some
turn up their noses.

No one can make
you unhappy
without
your consent.

Did is a word
of achievement,
Won't is a word
of retreat,
Might is a word
of bereavement,
Can't is a word
of defeat,
Ought is a word
of duty,
Try is a word
each hour,
Will is a word
of beauty,
Can is a word
of power.

*It takes
72 muscles to frown
and
only 14 to smile.*

*A great pleasure
in life is doing
what people say
you cannot do.*

...Walter Gagehot

If at first
you do succeed,
try not
to act surprised.

*Don't be
afraid
to take
a big step.
You can't
cross
a chasm
in
two small jumps.*

...David Lloyd George

*The person
rowing the boat
seldom has time
to rock it.*

Things turn out the best for the people who make the best out of the way things turn out.

…Art Linkletter

*He who walks
in another's tracks
leaves
no footprints.*

…Joan Brannon

Be yourself.
Who else
is better qualified?

…Frank Giblin II

*Just because
it's common sense
doesn't mean
it's common
practice.*

*If you
question
whether
every day is
a great day—
try missing a few
and you'll find out.*

*The measure of success is
not whether you have
a tough problem
to deal with, but whether
it's the same problem
you had last year.*

...John Foster Dulles

*What most of us need
is more horsepower
and less exhaust.*

*I find
the greatest thing
in this world
is not so much
where we stand
as in what
direction
we are moving.*

…Oliver Wendell Holmes

*If you've made up
your mind you can do
something
you're absolutely right.*

*Rainbows
apologize
for angry skies.*

...*Sylvia A. Voirol*

*Never confuse
activity
with productivity.*

*Don't wait
for your ship
to come in,
swim out to it.*

I will go anywhere provided it is forward.

…David Livingstone

People are always blaming
their circumstances
for what they are.
I don't believe in circumstances.
The people who get on in this world
are the people who get up and look
for the circumstances they want,
and if they can't find them,
make them.

...George Bernard Shaw
"Mrs. Warren's Profession"

*Progress always
involves risk;
you can't steal
second base
and keep your foot
on first.* ...Frederick Wilcox

Most smiles are started

by another smile.

The difference between
ordinary
and extraordinary
is that little extra.

Life works

if you

work at it!

*A pat on the back
is only a few vertebrae
removed from a kick
in the pants, but is miles
ahead in results.*

...V. Wilcox

Don't worry about the driver, just load up the wagon.

*May your ceilings
always be high
and your visibility
unlimited.*

If at first
you do succeed,
no one will believe
how hard
the job was.

*Master yourself
and
you can master
anything.*

...Ancient Proverb

When pulling a sled,
unless you are
the lead dog,
all of the scenery
looks the same.

All of us intend
to do better tomorrow,
and we would, too;
if we started now!

Luck is what happens when preparation meets opportunity.

…Elmer Letterman

If your efforts are sometimes greeted with indifference, don't lose heart— the sun puts on a wonderful show at daybreak, yet most of the people in the audience go on sleeping. ...Eda F. Teixeira

Time flies;
but remember
you
are the navigator.

One of these days
is
none of these days.

*People may doubt
what you say,
but they will believe
what you do.*

*Even when
opportunity knocks,
you still must
get out of your chair
to open the door.* ...Nuggets

Average is like having one foot in ice water and one foot in scalding water— on the average you're comfortable!

*You can't turn back
the clock
but you can
wind it up again.*

...Bonnie Prudden

You!

You are the person
who has to decide
whether you'll do it,
or toss it aside.
You are the person
who makes up
your mind
whether you'll lead
or linger behind.
Whether you'll try
for a goal that is far
or be contented to stay
where you are.
Take it or leave it,
there's something to do
just think it over—
It's all up to you!

A diamond is
a piece of coal
that
stuck to the job.

He who hesitates—

gets bumped

from behind.

*Some people watch
the parade go by;
Others march in it.
You be the grand marshal.*

*A ship in a harbor
is safe,
but that's not what
ships are built for.*

*A smile
increases
your
face value.*

*It's nice to work
with friendly people.
Be one.*

Good, better, best;
Never rest
Till "good"
be "better"
and "better" best.

...Mother Goose

*Here's hoping
you'll have lots
to smile about
always!*

USE THIS CONVENIENT ORDER FORM FOR ADDITIONAL
COPIES OF ALL THE KAPLAN BOOKS

NAME _____

ADDRESS _____

CITY _____

STATE _____ ZIP CODE _____

I WOULD LIKE TO ORDER:

_____ CHEERS BOOKS @ $5.95

_____ SMILES BOOKS @ $5.95

_____ FRIENDS BOOKS @ $5.95

_____ HAPPINESS BOOKS @ $5.95

_____ THANKS BOOKS @ $5.95

_____ 3 BOOK SETS WITH SLIP COVER @ $17.50
(CHEERS, SMILES, FRIENDS)

PLEASE SEND ORDER FORM AND CHECK OR MONEY ORDER
TO: **CHEERS, P.O. BOX 550513, ATLANTA, GA. 30355-3013**

USE THIS CONVENIENT ORDER FORM FOR ADDITIONAL
COPIES OF ALL THE KAPLAN BOOKS

NAME _____

ADDRESS _____

CITY _____

STATE _____ ZIP CODE _____

I WOULD LIKE TO ORDER:

_____ CHEERS BOOKS @ $5.95

_____ SMILES BOOKS @ $5.95

_____ FRIENDS BOOKS @ $5.95

_____ HAPPINESS BOOKS @ $5.95

_____ THANKS BOOKS @ $5.95

_____ 3 BOOK SETS WITH SLIP COVER @ $17.50
(CHEERS, SMILES, FRIENDS)

PLEASE SEND ORDER FORM AND CHECK OR MONEY ORDER
TO: **CHEERS, P.O. BOX 550513, ATLANTA, GA. 30355-3013**